Growing Up With Technology

Computer Concepts for the Young Mind

Elementary Prime Edition

Emmanuel Clarke

Clarke Publishing and Consulting Group, Inc.

CP&CG

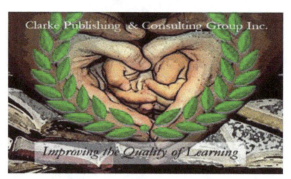

Growing Up with Technology

Elementary Prime Edition
First Edition

Emmanuel Clarke

President/CEO
Emmanuel Clarke
Author and Professor

Vice President
Miatta Stella Herring
School Publishing & Marketing

Managing Editor
Michael Dundas

Visual Artist
Laura Cuevas

Sales and Marketing Rep.
Mustapha Kallon

Senior Production Editor
Candrick Clarke

Graphic Artist
Oudvin Cassell

Senior Market Analyst
Jonathan Reeves

To All Parents and Children,

As Liberia has once again found itself at the crossroad of its educational renaissance, we all need to play our parts in helping our children learn in this digital age. Unlike ten years ago, technology or computer technology is now an integral part of everyday learning, and Liberia is no exception to this ideology. Keeping up with the rapid advances in technology can be challenging. At Clarke Publishing and Consulting Group, Inc., we understand technology's role in the world around us, but also the importance of educating young children in postwar Liberia about the world of technology. Therefore, we have developed a curriculum designed to instruct students on the fundamentals of computer technology and application. The concepts behind each application will be introduced and will be followed by activities using the parts of a computer, keyboarding, drawing applications, and Internet.

This curriculum will introduce your child to use the technology beginning in first grade continuing through fifth grade. It will be part of your child's regular school work and will enhance the other subjects your child is studying with cross-curricular activities. Due to the fact that the Liberian civil conflict threw our kids several decades behind, we all need to work together in helping them bridge this learning gap or digital divide.

Among the many benefits that your child will receive from this curriculum, the most important benefit is that your child will have a strong foundation in computer technology that will be increasingly important through each stage of your child's life. From a survey Clarke Publishing and Consulting Group, Inc. conducted in 2010, found that kids in Liberian schools are excited most, when it comes to learning about computer technology and its applications. Our survey also found that the Internet and the World Wide Web are the two most favorites applications loved by Liberian school children.

Of course, we could not facilitate the education of your young child without your help. Parents and guardians are truly the first and most important educators in a young child's life.

If you have any further questions, suggestions or concerns, please feel free to contact your child's teacher directly. If he or she cannot address your questions or concerns please feel free to contact us through the following means:
Our Web site at, www.clarkepublish.com once on our home page, click on the contact link for our local office phone numbers: 0886-103-907 or e-mail: info@clarkepublish.com

Sincerely,
Elementary School Editorial Staff
Clarke Publishing and Consulting Group, Inc.

Preface

The Clarke Publishing and Consulting Group Technology Learning Series® offers the finest textbook in computer and technical education to our Liberian students. This book is the answer to the many requests I have received from the Ministry of Education, instructors, students and education authorities in Liberia for a textbook that provides a succinct, yet thorough, introduction to computers at the elementary school level. The need for elementary teachers to teach essential technology skills to their students is our reason for the creation of the *Growing Up with Technology* series. These books continue with the innovation, quality, and reliability that educators have come to expect from Clarke Publishing and Consulting Group.

In *Growing Up with Technology: Elementary Prime Edition,* you will find an educationally sound, highly visual, and easy-to-follow pedagogy that presents a complete, yet to the point, treatment of introductory computer subjects. Because our primary business at Clarke Publishing and Consulting Group, Inc., we develop the perfect technology education program that starts students with the basics and gradually builds their skill sets. Through interesting lessons, activities, and projects, the *Growing Up with Technology series* is able to present elementary-aged students with core computing concepts and applications essential for future success while having fun!

Overview

Growing Up with Technology introduces our Liberian elementary-aged children to the basics of computers and computer applications. This textbook is organized into five chapters that cover:

- What Is A Computer
- Getting Started with the Computer
- Graphics, Files, and Folders
- The Internet
- The Keyboard

Organization of the Textbook

The *Growing Up with Technology* textbooks are organized so that the material is presented in chapters that start with an overview of what concepts students will learn, provide instruction and hands-on reinforcement, and conclude with end-of-chapter activities. With colorful illustrations, clear diagrams, and succinct step-by-step activities, our textbooks create a successful learning environment for students.

Visually Stimulating Presentation the book's cast of Liberian characters visually engage young learners while introducing valuable technology skills. Students will follow two characters' (Baby E and Eukey) journey through each level, making it fun for them to learn the concepts presented. In addition, Baby E and Eukey, are helpful characters, provide insight, positive reinforcement, and assistance in the form of marginal notes through the texts.

Good things come in smaller packages

In this text, Baby E and Eukey accompany students through each chapter

Flexibility Student lessons combine basic technology concepts with hands-on, step-by-step activities. These textbooks are designed so that students can work independently and in groups. *Growing Up with Technology* can also be used in a variety of classroom settings:

- **Lab Setting** A classroom with one-to-one correlation between students and computers.
- **Classroom with Shared Computer** A standard classroom with small groups of students required to share a computer. Like the learning situations we're faced with here in Liberia, students rotate using computer to complete the lesson.
- **Classroom with Teacher Aides** Classroom with a teacher as well as a teacher aide. The teacher aide can instruct one or more students at time.

Chapter Overview Well-structured student activities can make the difference between students merely participating in a class and retaining the information they learn. Using color-coded headings, teachers and students can determine when they are learning computer concepts in the blue section, when it's time for hands-on activities in the yellow section, or when they are working independently on the end-of-chapter material in the lime-green section.

About the Author

Emmanuel Clarke, AAS, BS, MSc, MSc, OCP, PM

Emmanuel is currently the President and CEO of Clarke Publishing and Consulting Group, Inc., a textbook publishing company he started in 2007. Emmanuel is also a faculty member at Mercer County Community College in Trenton NJ, Burlington County College in Burlington New Jersey, and the United Methodist University in Monrovia, Liberia. He holds a B.S. in Engineering from the New Jersey Institute of Technology, NJIT, a Master's in Information System, and another Master's in Project Management from this same institution. He also holds an AAS in Computer Programming from Mercer County Community College and a Certificate in Project Management (PM) from this same institution. Mr. Clarke holds a certificate in Instruction and Curriculum Design and Development from Langevin Learning Services. He is current pursuing a doctorate in Human Centered Computing from the New Jersey Institute of Technology.

Clarke holds several professional certificates which include: Oracle Certified Professional (OCP)

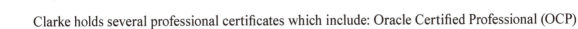

from Oracle University and Training Center in NYC, Certified Information Systems Implementer from NJIT, and a Certificate in Customer Service Trainer from the State of New Jersey Division of Human Services.

After a successful career working for the State of New Jersey Department of Health and Human Services, Child Care Networks and Mental Health Agencies as a MIS Director and Database Analyst as well as doing consultant work for Bullrun Financial LLC, a subsidiary of Merrill Lynch as a Financial Data Analyst and Bank of America as a Quality Control Special Representative, Emmanuel finally finds that his true calling was education. He has been teaching since 2005 at Mercer County Community College as well as training the college's corporate clients in various applications software. Clarke is also an Adjunct Information Technology Professor at Burlington County College in New Jersey.

Emmanuel serves on the Mercer County Community College Advisor Commission on Information Technology. He is a Distinguished Lecturer and does corporate training for companies such as: Bristol-Myers Squibb, the State of New Jersey Department of Banking and Insurance, Educational Testing Service, ETS, Firmenich, just to name a few. He loves singing, reading, running, hacking, fishing, making new friends, sleeping and bunchy jumping. He is the author of more than fourteen books, "The Fraternal Deception", "In Tears and Blood", "The City of Hopeless Romantics", "How the West Lost Africa to China: A Critical Analysis of Western Exploitation and China's Emerging Opportunities (to be released 2014)", "Computer Concepts for Liberian Schools" (currently being used by the Ministry of Education and schools in Liberia), "Growing Up With Technology, Primary Edition", "Computer Lab Manual For Elementary Schools", " Computer Lab Manual For Jr. High", " Computer Lab Manual For Sr. High", "Project Management for a Modern Liberia", "Management Information Systems for Liberian Colleges and Universities", "Computer Concepts for Liberian Colleges and Universities", "Computer Lab for Colleges and Universities", "So Far to Run (ghost wrote)" just to name a few.

Acknowledgements

The Clarke Publishing and Consulting Group, CP&CG Technology Learning Series would not be the leading computer education series without the contributions of outstanding publishing professionals. As always, we would like to thank all those who spent hundreds of hours in helping us bring this book to a successful completion. I would like to thank the staff at Clarke Publishing and Consulting Group, Inc. for their invaluable service to this one of a kind organization.

Finally, I could never have written this book without the loving support of my family. my four loving children, Regina (Baby E), Eukey, Emmaree, Emmanuella, and my partner in romance, Wante Mekey Saygbe. Thanks for making the sacrifices (mostly in time not spent with me) to permit me to make this dream into reality.

My heartfelt thanks go to the hard working instructional designers at McGraw Hill for their guidance during the development of this book, it was quite a learning experience. Thanks to Samuel H. Taylor for inspiring me during my information technology career journey in the U.S.

This book wouldn't have been completed had it not been for the inputs from computer teachers at various schools in Liberia, staff at the Ministry of Education, Curriculum and Texbook Division, especially Esther Mulbah, and instructors at various public and private institutions around the nation. Thanks for your insight, I listened and I have come to deliver as promised. I would have been running in circle hadn't it been for David Sewon of the Monrovia Consolidate School System, MCSS, and John Gbozee of the University of Liberia, J. Frederick Clarke, and my two mothers, Regina W. Gaye, and Twon Bowo Clarke, for constantly praying for me. Thank to my many friends and admirers for your moral support. And to those unsung contributors that made this project possible, I owe you my gratitude.

Table of Contents

The symbol on 'Preface' is 9 using Roman numberls

Table of Contents

Chapter 2
Getting Started with the Computer

Table of Contents

Chapter 3
Graphics, Files, and Folders

Table of Contents

Chapter 4

The Internet

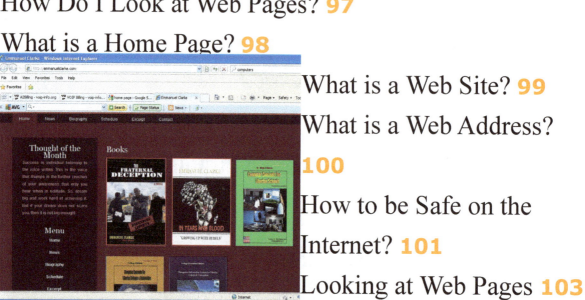

Table of Contents

Chapter 5
The Keyboard

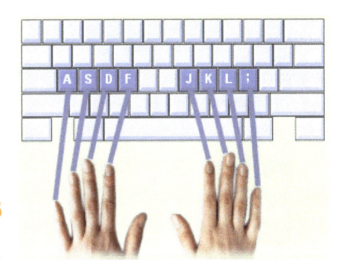

CHAPTER 1

The Computer

New Words

CD	monitor
CD Drive	program
CD-ROM Drive	software
Data	speaker
Hardware	system unit

What You Will Learn

 Computer-------------------Computer----------------------Computer

 Keyboard--------------------Keyboard----------------------Keyboard

 Mouse----------------------------Mouse----------------------------Mouse

 Printer--------------------Printer-----------------------Printer

 Screen----------------------Screen-----------------------Screen

Words You May Know

You will learn about computer.

You will learn the parts of a computer.

You will learn about software.

You will learn rules to help you use a computer.

FIGURE 1-1 Baby E reflects on what She Knows and what will she will learn from the book.

FIGURE 1-2 Students in a computer lab doing their work. Like boys, girls too love working with the computer in Liberia.

Why Learn About Computers?

Computers are all around you.

Computers are in schools.

Computers are in homes.

Computers are at work.

FIGURE 1-3 I Say Hello to a world of possibilities once computer knowledge is acquired

FIGURE 1-4 Computer is now a big part of learning in school.

FIGURE 1-5 Computer is find in many offices in Liberia

FIGURE 1-6 Computer is also used in home around the world.

Why Learn About Computers?

Computers can help you learn.

Computers can help you draw.

Computers can help you write.

Computers can even help you communicate.

Computers can even help you play.

Have you used a computer?

FIGURE 1-7 Computer can help you do a lot of things that your parents couldn't do when they were in school. In fact, the computer has changed the way students learn and communicate.

What is a Computers?

A **computer** is an electronic machine.

A computer operates under **commands** or Instructions.

A computer works with data.

Data are words, number, or pictures.

You enter data into a computer.

The computer is a very amazing piece of machine, friends!

FIGURE 1-8 The computer is so amazing that you can use it to do almost anything.

What are the Parts of a Computer?

A Computer has many Parts.

The parts of a computer are called **hardware**.

Some computer have as many as 25 different parts.

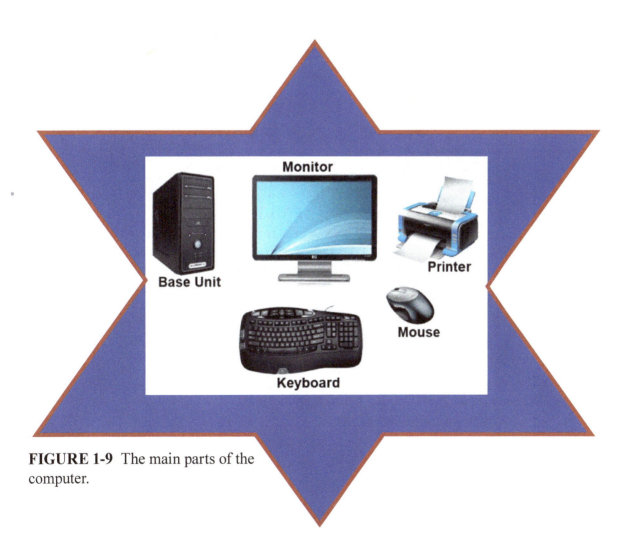

FIGURE 1-9 The main parts of the computer.

What are the Parts of a Computer?

A **system unit** is hardware.

It does the work.

A system unit has many parts.

You cannot see the parts.

The parts work together.

FIGURE 1-10 The System Unit of a Computer. The System Unit is contains all the electronic parts for the computer. It is like the him head the contains the brain.

FIGURE 1-11 Luah is holding a CD-ROM in her hand. The CD goes into the CD-ROM Drive on the System Unit.

What are the Parts of a Computer?

A **monitor** shows you words.

A monitor shows you pictures.

A monitor looks like a TV.

You look at the **screen**.

Students in Liberia use their monitor to watch movies and to play games

FIGURE 1-12 A computer monitor showing the author in a Microsoft Word Document. A monitor can be used for so many things like, watching movies, Playing games, or doing work.

What are the Parts of a Computer?

A computer has a Keyboard.

A **Keyboard** helps you write.

You press keys to type letters.

You press keys to type numbers.

You type to tell the computer what to do.

Look! Baby E typed her name and drew a face.

A keyboard does many things," says Baby E

Baby E

FIGURE 1-13 A Keyboard is a primary input device. This means, it is one of the first devices that a user uses to enter data and instructions into the computer.

What are the Parts of a Computer?

A computer has a **mouse**.

This is a computer mouse.

This is a computer mouse, too.

Each picture is a computer mouse.

FIGURE 1-14 Different types of computer mouse that are used to trigger an event or enter data or instructions into the computer. Mice is the plural for mouse.

"This is not a computer mouse."
Says, Eukey

FIGURE 1-15 Eukey holding a mouse in his hands. Not all computers come with a mouse. For example, notebook, laptop, tablet PCs, etc.

What are the Parts of a Computer?

A computer has **CD-ROM drive**.

A CD-ROM drive is part of the system unit.

A CD-ROM drive is also called a **CD- drive.**

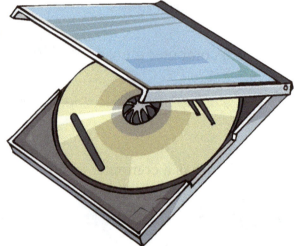

FIGURE 1-16 A CD-ROM that is used for storing data and information, programs and music as well as other important files.

A CD drive uses a **CD**.

You put a CD in a CD drive.

A CD drive reads the data on a CD.

You can also put a special type of CD call **DVD** into some CD drive.

FIGURE 1-17 A CD Drive that can read data and instruction from a CD as well as write data and instructions to a CD.

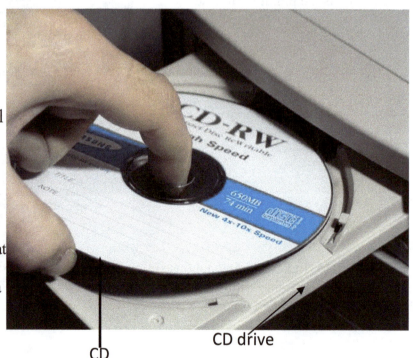

CD

CD drive

What are the Parts of a Computer?

A **speaker** plays sounds.

Sounds can be words.

Sounds can be music.

Sounds can be noise.

Sounds can also be data.

FIGURE 1-18 A pictorial of what the speaker of a computer does. As you can see, the speaker makes sound from the computer. It allows you to hear music from a CD and other media files.

What are the Parts of a Computer?

A **printer** writes words on paper.

A printer writes numbers on paper.

A printer puts pictures on paper.

Have you ever used a printer?

FIGURE 1-19 A printer produces a hard-copy of a document that we see on the monitor or screen. The above image drawn by Baby-E can be printed by the printer on the right.

What is Software?

Software tells the computer what to do.

Software is also called **programs**.

Games on a computer are software.

Paint programs are software

Microsoft Word is also a software.

FIGURE 1-20 Various types of computer software or programs. A computer program tells the computer what to do and how to do those things you want the computer to do.

Why Follow Computer Rules?

Everyone must follow **rules.**

Some rules protect the computer.

Some rules protect you.

Computer rules are easy to follow.

Does everyone follow the rules here in Liberia?

What happens if you do not follow rules?

FIGURE 1-21 It is good to ask for help when using the computer. Tips for using the computer as students before becoming technology savvy.

> Every computer user must follow rules, says Baby-E

FIGURE 1-22 Baby-E telling Spot as well as you to always follow rules when using the computer.

Why Follow Computer Rules?

Here are some rules you can follow:

1. Make sure grown up knows when you are using a computer

2. Always ask when you need help.

3. Always search use bing.com or google.com to find information

4. Use the Ministry of Education website for information as well.

FIGURE 1-23 Students in a computer lab at the G.W. Gibson High School in Monrovia.

FIGURE 1-24 Students in a computer lab at the Child Development Academy, CDA in Monrovia.

5. Hold CD on its sides.

6. Do not eat or drink when you are using a computer.

7. Keep magnets away from the computer. Do you know other computer rules?

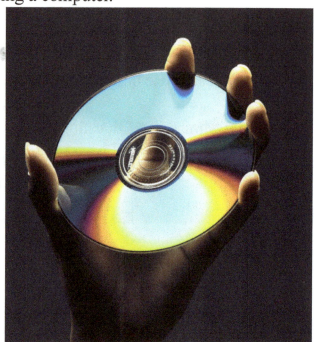

FIGURE 1-25 Students need to follow these basic rules as illustrated or shown in these pictures

Matching

Match the words to the pictures.

1. monitor

2. keyboard

3. mouse

4. printer

5. speaker

6. system unit

7. CD-ROM

8. software

CHAPTER 2

Getting Started
With the Computer

New Words

button	icon
click	menu
drag	mouse pad
pointer	toolbar

Words You May Know

Exit-----------------------------------**Exit**-------------------------------------Exit

Paint----------------------------------**Paint**-------------------------------------Paint

Mouse----------------------------------**Mouse**-----------------------------Mouse

Program-------------------**Program**------------------Program

Quit--------------------------**Quit**--------------------------Quit

Start--------------------------**Start**----------------------------Start

Words You Will Learn

You will learn how to use a mouse

You will learn how to use a menu.

You will learn how to use a toolbar.

The Mouse

You use a mouse to tell the computer what to do.

The mouse is next to your computer.

The mouse is on a **mouse pad.**

You move the mouse around on the mouse pad.

The mouse is an input device.

FIGURE 2-1 A computer mouse allows a user to enter data or instruction into the computer. It is one of the primary devices of the computer.

FIGURE 2-2 Baby-E scribbles .on her work-sheet with her pencil. With a computer and a mouse, she can perform the same task in Microsoft Paint

The Mouse

A mouse can have one button.

A mouse can have two buttons.

Place your right hand on the mouse.

Put your index finger on the left mouse

button or on the one mouse button.

FIGURE 2-3 Two different types of mice: the top mouse is a mechanical mouse and bottom mouse is an optical mouse.

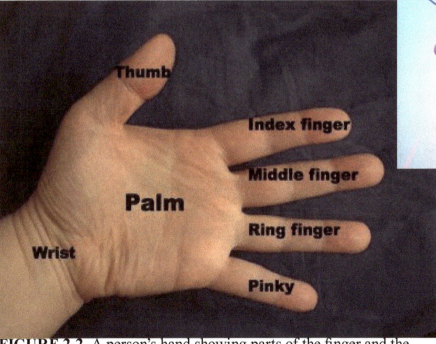

FIGURE 2-2 A person's hand showing parts of the finger and the parts of the hand.

The Mouse

Move the mouse on the mouse pad.

The **pointer** moves on the screen.

Move the mouse up.

The pointer moves up.

Move the mouse down.
The pointer moves down.

FIGURE 2-3 The mouse pointer can be many shapes, it allows computer users to do many things on the screen or monitor.

The Mouse

You use the mouse to **click**.

You tap button to click.

A click tells the computer what to do
Double-click means to fast clicks—click click

Practice double-clicking by tapping your fingers on your desk in a tap-tap—stop—tap-tap—stop pattern.

FIGURE 2-4 Direction on how to click and double click a mouse.

FIGURE 2-5 Baby-E telling you how to double click the mouse. Can you follow her instruction on how to double click

The Mouse

Icons are small pictures on your screen.

You click some icons.

You double-click some icons.

Clicking an icon tells the computer what to do.

FIGURE 2-6 Eukey has an icon in his hands. Can you find icon on your computer like Eukey did?

FIGURE 2-7 A screen showing several icons on the desktop. Some people desktop can have several dozen icons.

The Mouse

You can us the mouse to **drag**.

Drag means to move an object from one place to another place on the screen.

You can drag icons.

FIGURE 2-8 Picture of Baby-E's dog, Spot. If this picture was an icon on the desktop it could be moved by dragging and dropping it into a folder.

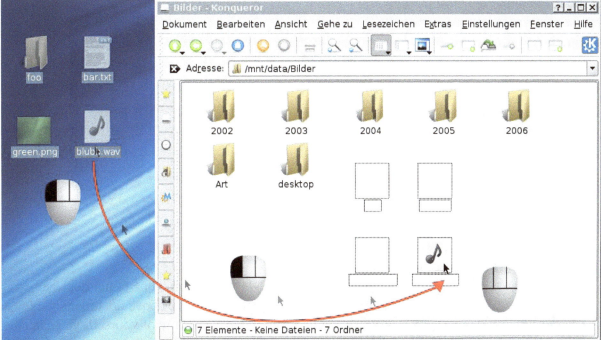

FIGURE 2-9 A screenshot showing how to drag an icon from the desktop into a folder using a computer mouse. Can you practice doing this? If you practice, it will become easy for you.

The Mouse

A **menu** is a list of words.

Programs have menus.

You click a menu name to open the menu.

You click a word on the menu to tell the computer what to do.

FIGURE 2-10 A screenshot of the menu items of Paint. Do you see the various menu items on the right?

FIGURE 2-11 Baby-E and one of her dogs having fun. Their picture is in the above document being edited. If you have a picture of yourself, you can edit or change the way it looks using Microsoft Paint or any kind of photo editing software or program.

Toolbars

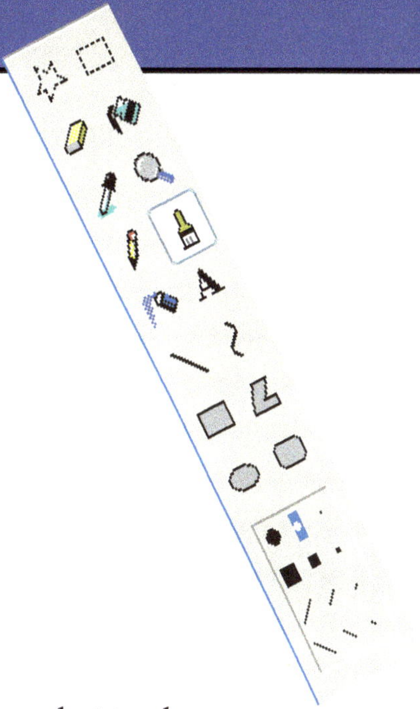

Programs have toolbars.

A **toolbar** is a group of tools.

Each tool is a **button** on the toolbar.

A button is like an icon.

Some buttons have pictures on them.

Some buttons have words on them.

You click a button to tell the. computer what to do.

FIGURE 2-12 A Paint toolbar showing many tools found in the software.

FIGURE 2-13 A picture of Eu-key and his sister, Baby-E along with their do.

Using the Mouse

You use a mouse to tell the computer what to do.

You use the mouse to point.

You use the mouse to click.

You use the mouse to drag.

What You Will Do

You will move the mouse

You will point.

You will drag.

You will double—click to start Paint

FIGURE 2-14 Students in a computer lab at the Child Development Academy, CDA in Monrovia using the computer mouse to do their lab work.

Using the Mouse

To Move the Pointer

GO **1.** Put the mouse on the mouse pad. See the pointer on the screen.

2. Move the mouse toward you on the mouse pad.

See the pointer move down the screen.

3. Move the mouse away from you on the mouse pad.

See the pointer move up the screen.

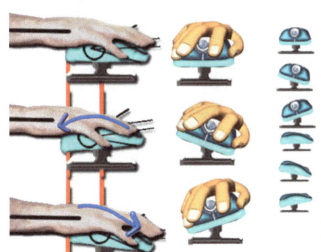

FIGURE 2-15 A pictorial illustration on how to mover the mouse. Practice these moves that will help you.

Using the Mouse

4. Move the mouse to the left.

See the pointer moves to the left.

5. Move the mouse to the right.

See the pointer moves to the right.

You use the mouse to move the pointer.

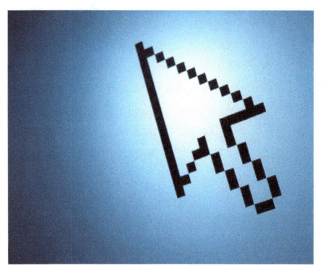

FIGURE 2-16 A picture of the pointer of a mouse. the mouse pointer can be changed into any shape.

FIGURE 2-17 Let Eukey show you how to move the mouse pointer left and right and win a price from your teacher.

Using the Mouse

To Point to an Icon

 1. Move the mouse to point to.

The icon changes when the pointer is on it.

 2. Move the pointer off.

3. Move the mouse to point to other icons on the desktop.

You used the mouse to point. STOP

You can point to any icon on the screen.

FIGURE 2-18 Try pointing the mouse to the Microsoft Paint Program. Just like Baby-E does when she wants to use that program.

Using the Mouse

To Drag an Icon

 1. Move the mouse to point to.

2. Press the left mouse button and hold the button down.

3. Move the mouse to drag the icon across the screen.

FIGURE 2-19 A picture of a 2nd Grader, name, Emmaree using the computer mouse on a desktop computer.

4. Lift your finger from the mouse button.

You used the mouse to drag the icon.

Using the Mouse

To Double—Click and Start Paint

GO **1.** Move the mouse to point to.

2. Double—click the left mouse button.

You used the mouse to start the Paint program! **STOP**

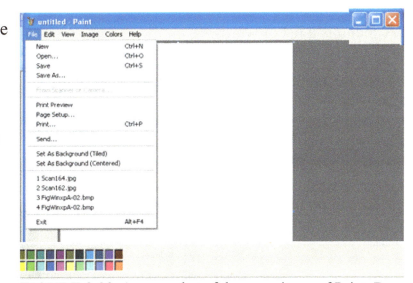

FIGURE 2-20 A screenshot of the menu items of Paint. Do you see the various menu items on the right?

FIGURE 2-21 A picture of a 2nd Grader, name, Emmaree using the computer mouse on a laptop computer.

Viewing Menu

Most programs have menu bar.

The menu bar is at the top of a window.

When you point to a word on the menu bar, a menu opens.

A menu is a list of words.

You use a menu to tell the computer what to do.

What You Will Do

You will point to a menu bar.

You will click a on the menu bar.

FIGURE 2-22 A menu give users a list of things that lets the user tell the computer what to do.

Viewing Menu

GO **1.** Use the Menu to point to the word **File**.

2. Click the word **File**.

You see a list of words.

3. Point to the word **Edit.**

4. Point to the word **View**.

FIGURE 2-23 Baby-E and her dog Spot thinking about items found on a program menu.

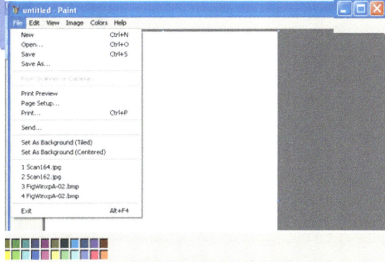

FIGURE 2-24 A menu has different items that allow a user to choose which item to apply or feature to a document.

Viewing Menu

5. Point to the word **Image**.

6. Point to the word **Colors**.

7. Point to the word **Help**.

8. Click the **blue bar** above the menu bar.

You used the mouse to open menus.

FIGURE 2-25 Baby-E draws the letter 'P' on a big poster sheet with here baby dog next to her.

Using the Toolbar Buttons

You click a toolbar button to pick a drawing tool.

You move the mouse to use a drawing tool.

You draw on the blank area on the screen.

The blank area is called a **canvas**.

What You Will Do

You will use toolbar buttons.

You will draw shapes.

FIGURE 2-26 Eukey loves using Microsoft Paint to draw pictures and shapes. Practice doing the same.

Using the Toolbar Buttons

To Use Toolbar Buttons

GO **1.** Click

2. Move the pointer to the canvas.

The pointer changes to

3. Click the yellow box.

4. Move  to the canvas, then click.

The canvas changes to yellow.

5. Click the white box.

Using the Toolbar Buttons

6. Move to the canvas, then click.

The canvas changes to white again.

FIGURE 2-27 A picture of a 2nd Grader, name, Emmaree using the computer mouse on a desktop computer to work in Microsoft Paint.

You used the mouse to click toolbar buttons and change the color of the canvas. **STOP**

Using the Toolbar Buttons

To Use the Brush Tool

GO **1.** Click

2. Click any color box.

3. Point to the canvas.

The pointer changes to ⌐⌐⌐

4. Point near the top of the canvas.

FIGURE 2-28 Using Microsoft Paint, you can change the color of Baby-E and her dog to your favorite color. What is your favorite color? Baby-E love blue.

Using the Toolbar Buttons

5. Press and hold the mouse button.

6. Drag ⌐|⌐ down.

7. Let go of the mouse button.

8. Move ⌐|⌐, then drag ⌐|⌐ to draw.

You used the Brush tool to draw.

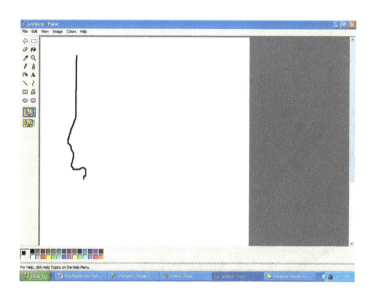

FIGURE 2-29 Using Microsoft Paint, you can draw a line of any shape, size and color. Eukey knows how to draw a color line, can you try drawing a color line?

Using the Toolbar Buttons

To Use the Brush Tool

GO **1.** Click

2. Point to the canvas

The pointer changes  to

3. Click the **red box**.

4. Move pointer to the top
of the canvas.

5. Press and hold the
mouse button.

FIGURE 2-30 Using Microsoft
Paint, you can change the handler
color to any color of your choice just
Eukey and his sister, Baby-E do.

Using the Toolbar Buttons

6. Drag right

7. Let go of the mouse button.

> You used the Line tool to draw a red line.

8. Click a new color, move, then

drag to draw a different

color line.

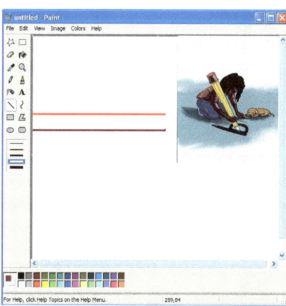

FIGURE 2-31 Using Microsoft Paint and the mouse, you can draw lines of any color size and shape of your choice.

Using the Toolbar Buttons

To Create Shapes

GO **1.** Click

2. Point to the middle of the canvas, press and hold the mouse button.

3. Drag ⫟ down and to the right, then let go of the mouse button.

You made a shape with four sides.

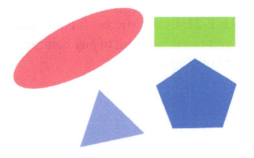

FIGURE 2-32 Using Microsoft Paint and the mouse, you can draw many different types of shapes of any color and size of your choice.

Using the Toolbar Buttons

4. Click

5. Point to a space under your shape, press and hold the mouse button.

6. Drag ⌐¦¬ to the right, then let go of the mouse button.

You made a round shape. **STOP**

FIGURE 2-33 Using Microsoft Paint and the mouse, you can draw many different types of shapes of any color and size of your choice. Is Baby-E saying the truth? If Yes, try it yourself.

Using the Toolbar Buttons

To Use the Eraser Tool

1. Click

2. Point to the round shape you drew and hold

down the mouse button.

3. Drag the pointer over the shape, then let go of

the mouse button. You erased a shape.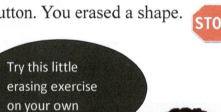

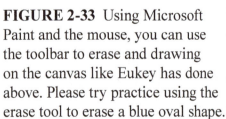

Try this little erasing exercise on your own

FIGURE 2-33 Using Microsoft Paint and the mouse, you can use the toolbar to erase and drawing on the canvas like Eukey has done above. Please try practice using the erase tool to erase a blue oval shape.

Matching

Match the words to the pictures.

1. pointer

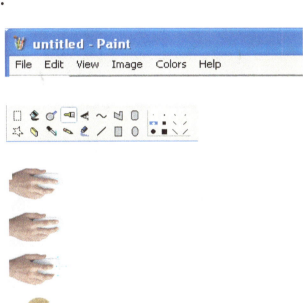

2. menu bar

3. Paint icon

4. toolbar

5. Click

CHAPTER 3

Graphics, Files, and Folders

New Words

file	graphic
file name	save
folder	scroll
	window

Words You May Know

button----------------------button------------------------button

CD-------------------------CD---------------------------CD

click----------------------------click------------------------------click

menu-------------------------menu--------------------------menu

system unit---------------system unit--------------system unit

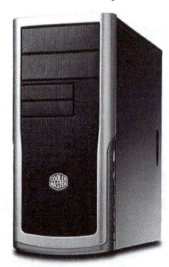

What You Will Learn

You will learn about graphics.

You will learn about files.

You will learn about folders.

You will learn about windows.

What Are Graphics?

A **graphic** can be a shape

A graphic can be a picture

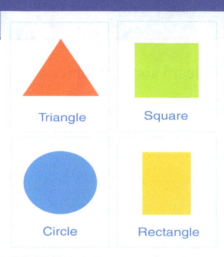

FIGURE 3-1 Images of various geometric shapes. These are also called graphics.

FIGURE 3-2 The tree on the left is also called a graphic. Can you name some graphics?

A graphic can be a photograph.

FIGURE 3-3 This beautify photograph is also called a graphic.

What Are Graphics?

You can see graphics on a computer.

You can see graphics that you made.

You can see graphics that somebody else made.

What graphics do you see when you use a computer?

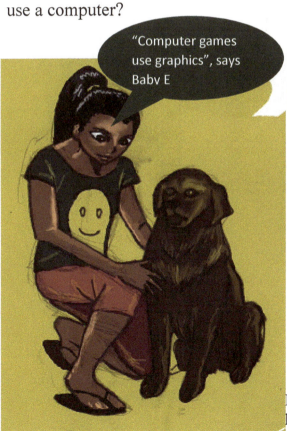

"Computer games use graphics", says Baby E

FIGURE 3-4 This beautify illustration of a teacher in her classroom is also called a graphic.

FIGURE 3-5 This this image of Baby-E and her dog is a graphic.

What Are Graphics?

A graphic can be a digital photograph.

You can take a photograph with a digital

You can use a computer to see

I always use a digital camera to take pictures of my family

FIGURE 3-6 A picture of a Nikon digital camera which belongs to Eukey is also called a graphic.

What Are Files?

Computers use **files**.

A file stores words.

A file stores numbers.

A file stores graphics.

A file stores sounds.

FIGURE 3-7 Pictures of various types of file. You see, whenever you store a picture, a sound, a bunch of numbers or letters into the computer the computer it stores them as a file. Since the computer is an electronic machine, it only understands binary language or '1 and 0' You will learn about data representation and binary number in the 7th Grade.

What is a Files Name

Each file has a name.

The name of the file is the **file name**.

The file name helps you find the file on the computer.

The picture of the tiger is a file.

The file name is "Tiger. jpg."

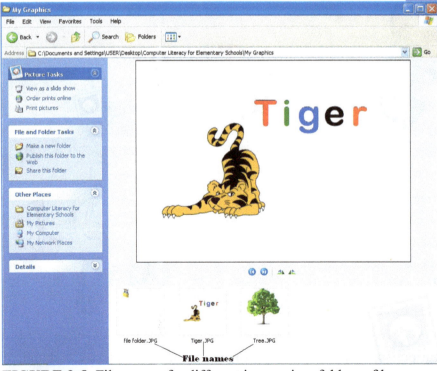

FIGURE 3-8 File names for different images in a folder. a file name has an extension. For example, these files have the extension of .JPG.

Can I Make a File?

You can make a graphic file when you use a computer.

Then you can **save** the graphic so you can access it anytime you want it.

When you save the graphic, you name it.

FIGURE 3-9 A picture of a 2ⁿᵈ Grader, name, Emmaree using the computer to save a file she created.

Baby E and Spot

FIGURE 3-10 File that is named 'Spot.jpg' being saved on a CD-ROM for ease of access in the future. Whenever you create a file to save, it is always a good idea to give it a name that you will remember.

Where are File Stored?

Files are stored on disks.

Files are stored on USB Flash drives.

Files are stored on CD-ROM discs.

Files are stores on the hard disk.

FIGURE 3-11 A picture of a Flash USB drive that allows users to save files onto it.

A hard disk drive is inside the system unit.

FIGURE 3-12 A picture of a computer hard drive that allows a user to save file on the computer for future access.

Where are File Found?

Files are on disks and drives.

When you want to use a file, the computer records the file on the disks.

When you want to save a file, the computer writes the file on the disk.

FIGURE 3-13 A picture showing how to put a CD-ROM into the CD-ROM drive of a computer

FIGURE 3-13 A picture Baby-E and here dog, Spot with several colorful CD-ROMs.

Where are File Stored?

Files are stored in **folders**.

You know that files have names.

Folders have names too!

You name folders so you can find them on a disk.

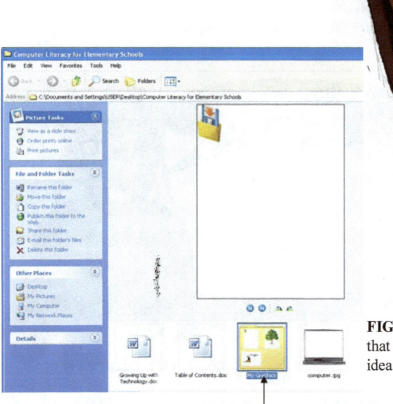

FIGURE 3-14 Folder is a container that stores computer files. It is a good idea to give your folder a name.

Folder name

How Do I Use a File?

To use a file, you open it.

The file opens in a **window**.

Look at the picture of Baby E below.

It shows Baby E file in a Paint window.

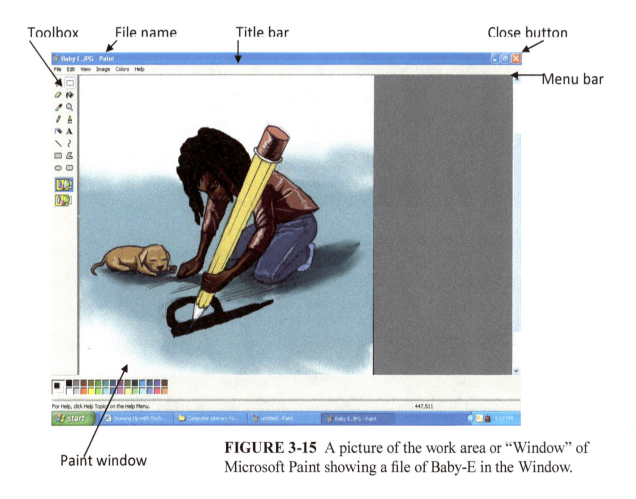

FIGURE 3-15 A picture of the work area or "Window" of Microsoft Paint showing a file of Baby-E in the Window.

How Do I Use a File?

You can **scroll** to see more of Babe E.

When you scroll, you use the scroll bars.

You can scroll up and down.

You can scroll left and right.

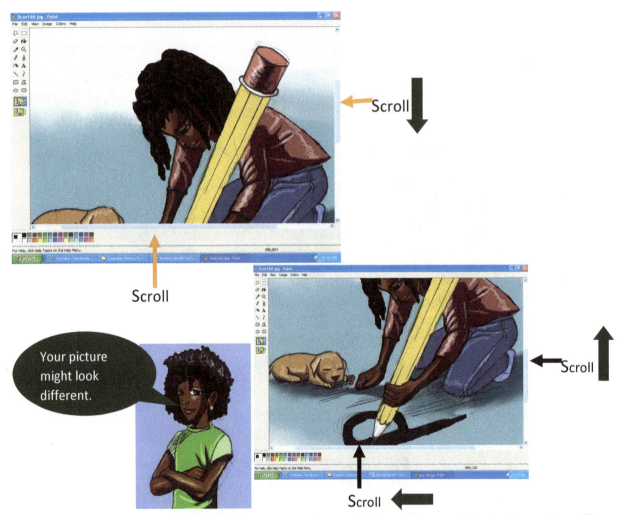

FIGURE 3-16 Illustration showing how to use the vertical scrollbar and the horizontal scrollbar in Microsoft Paint Window. Try practicing these scroll techniques.

Working with Files

A Graphic can be a picture.

You can save a graphic as a file.

You can give the file a file name.

A file can be saved on the computer.

What You Will Do

You will find a file.

You will open a file.

You will use scroll bars.

You will name and save a file.

When you are done using a file, you close it.

FIGURE 3-17 Eukey is informing you of one important thing you as a student should always do whenever you're using a file. Always close the file whenever you close it.

Working with Files

You can use Paint to draw.

You can use Paint to look at a picture.

To Start the Paint Program

GO **1.** Find ✑ on the desktop.

2. Double-click ✑

Paint starts.

Look at the new Paint window. **STOP**

FIGURE 3-18 Picture of an opened and Unsaved Paint windows with the toolbar on the left and the menu bar on the top.

Working with Files

Baby E too a picture of her dog.

The picture is saved on a disk.

To Open a File

The picture is a file.

To see the picture, you open the file.

To Open a File

GO **1.** Click **File** on the menu bar.

The File menu opens.

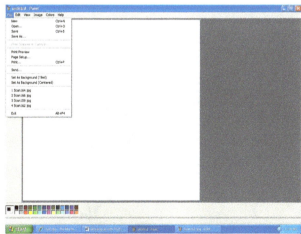

FIGURE 3-19 Picture of an opened and Unsaved Paint windows with the File Menu opened.

2. Click **Open**.

3. Find the file SpotTheDog.jpg.

4. Click the file name **SpotTheDog.jpg**.

5. Click **Open**.

The file opens

6. Click maximize button which is located in the upper right corner of the window.

The window is as big as it can get. STOP

FIGURE 3-20 Picture of Spot in an opened Paint window. Try using Microsoft Paint to edit or touchup an image file.

Using a Program

The File is open.

The file is very big.

You cannot see all of it.

What You Will Do

You will use the scroll bars.

You will change a file.

FIGURE 3-21 Picture of the scroll bar found in the windows of software programs.

FIGURE 3-22 Picture of students in their classroom learning History. This is a file you can change using Microsoft Paint.

Using a Program

Some pictures are too big to fit in the window.

You can **scroll** to see the rest of the picture.

What You Will Do

GO **1.** Drag the side scroll bar down.

You see more of Baby E.

FIGURE 3-23 Picture showing how to move the scroll bar down in order to bring into view an image of Baby-E and dog.

Using a Program

2. Drag the bottom **scroll bar** to the right →

FIGURE 3-24
Picture showing how to move the scroll bar right in order to bring into view an image of Baby-E and dog.

You will see more of Baby E

Using a Program

You can change a picture.

Then, you can give the file a new name.

After you name a file, you can save it.

To Change a File

GO **1.** Think of a way to change the dog picture.

You can draw a bow tie. You can draw a hat. How do you want to change the picture? Kids in Liberia love being creative when using a computer

Using a Program

2. Click a tool in the toolbox.

3. Use the too to draw on the dog picture.

You made a new graphic. STOP

FIGURE 3-25 Picture showing how to change or alter an image in Paint. Try changing a picture in Paint as well

Using a Program

You are done with the picture.

You want to keep the file.

What You Will Do

You will name and save the file.

You will close the file.

You will close the program.

FIGURE 3-26 Picture of Spot and Baby-E as she tells her dog the value in saving ones file once done working with it.

Saving and Closing

You can give the file a new file name.

You can save the file.

To Name and Save a File

GO **1.** Click **File** on the menu bar.

FIGURE 3-27 Picture of Spot in a Paint program window that is about to be save.

Saving and Closing

2. Click **Save As**.

A dialog box opens.

3. Type the file name.

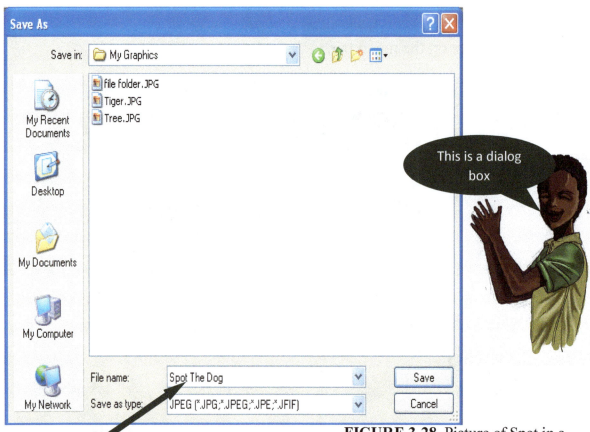

Type the new file name

FIGURE 3-28 Picture of Spot in a Paint program window that is saves as SpotTheDog.JPG.

Saving and Closing

4. Find the folder where you will save your file.

Click Save

You saved the file! **STOP**

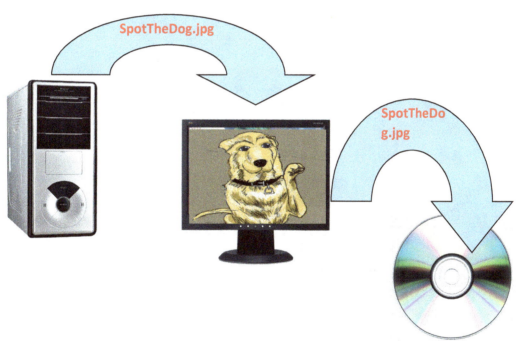

FIGURE 3-29 Picture showing how file called SpotTheDog is save to a CD-ROM for a future access by a user or anyone.

Saving and Closing

When you are done with a file, you close it.

The file is still on the computer.

When you close a file, you cannot use the file.

You cannot make changes to the file.

When you want to use the file again, you can open it.

FIGURE 3-30 A picture of a 2nd Grader, name, Emmaree saving a file and closing the program after using it. Can you try saving a file and closing a program?

Saving and Closing

When you are done with working with a program, you close it.

When you close a program, you cannot use the program.

The program is still on the computer.

You open the program when you want to use it again.

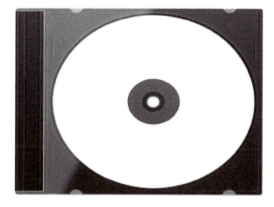

FIGURE 3-31 A picture of a CD-ROM with a saved file.

To Close a Program

1. Click

The Program is not running.

FIGURE 3-31 A picture of Baby-E and her dog, Spot.

Matching

Match the words to the pictures.

1. file name

2. folder

3. graphic

4. Scroll bars

CHAPTER 4

The Internet

New Words

file	graphic
file name	save
folder	scroll
	window

Words You May Know

Back…………………................…Back…......…………………….Back

program…………...............………..program…………….…………program

rules…………………................……rules………....……………….…..rules

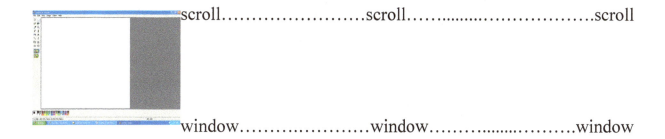

scroll…………………………scroll……............…………………scroll

window……………………window………….......…………window

What You Will Learn

You will learn about the Internet.

You will learn how to go online.

You will learn about e-mail.

You will learn about the Web.

You will learn how to be safe online.

FIGURE 4-1 A picture of students in the classroom during computer lab.

FIGURE 4-2 A picture of students in the classroom reading Liberian and African History..

What Is the Intern?

The **Internet** is a worldwide collection of computer Networks. The Internet connects computers.

Computers can work together.

Computers can share information. Kids in Liberia love the Internet.

The Internet has changed the way we learn.

These computers are connected, Spot

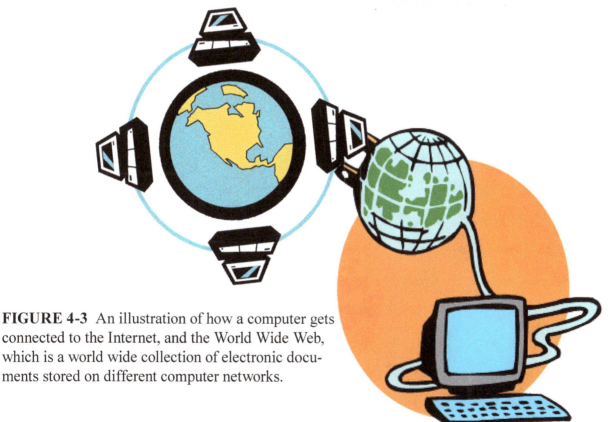

FIGURE 4-3 An illustration of how a computer gets connected to the Internet, and the World Wide Web, which is a world wide collection of electronic documents stored on different computer networks.

How Do I Use the Internet?

You go online to use the Internet

Online means you are on the Internet or

the Net as it it referred to in Liberia.

Some computers are always online.

Some computers are not always online

School kids in Liberia love to go online.

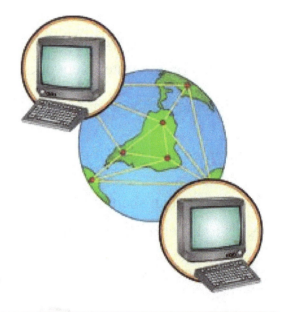

FIGURE 4-4 A picture of a computer connected to the Internet.

FIGURE 4-5 A picture of a 2nd grader, Emmaree, searching the Internet for her favorite Dress Up online game that lets little girls dress avatars with different clothing designs and make ups.

How Do I Go Online?

Some computers in parts of Africa dial—up to connect to the Internet.

Dial—up means your computer makes a call.

To make the call, the computer uses a modem.

A modem connects your computer to the Internet.

FIGURE 4-6 A picture showing the glob with the various continents. The Internet has made the world small than it appears. People can now communicate faster than the speed of light.

Currently in Liberia, you use a phone to call a friend. A computer uses a modem to call another computer.

FIGURE 4-7 An illustration of a young girl called Luah holding a CD-ROM in her hand with a dog in the background. What she said is the truth. Using a Dial-Up Modem is like using a cell phone to call another phone.

How Do I Go Online?

Sometimes, when you go online, you have to log on.

To log on, you may need a password.

A **password** is a secret word or numbers.

Once you are logged on, you can use e-mail, or the Web.

It is always a good practice to keep your password to yourself.

Do not share your password with your friends. Only share it with your parents.

FIGURE 4-8 A student on a computer using the Internet. Some websites require that you provide a password in order to log on for accessing resources on that website. Always keep your password secret. Do not share it with your friend.

Shhhh.....!!!!! Never tell anyone your computer password

FIGURE 4-9 Always keep your password secure. Your password should be a secret only you know. Baby-E never shares her password with her friend, only her parents know her password.

What is E-mail?

You can send mail over the Internet

Mail you send over the Internet is called **e-mail.**

E-mail is a short form for electronic mail.

To send an e-mail, you need an e-mail program.

Kids in Liberia love to send e-mails to their friends and family.

FIGURE 4-10 A a picture of a 2nd Grader, Emmaree on her computer sending an E-mail.

What is E-mail?

To send an e-mail, you need an e-mail address.

To get an e-mail, you need an e-mail address.

An e-mail address looks like this:

support@clarkepublishe.com or this:

wehtee@yahoo.com

FIGURE 4-11 A student in an Internet cafe in Bolahun Liberia, sending an e-mail.

An e-mail address tells the computer where to send the e-mail.

Many kids in Liberia have e-mail address to communicate with family and friend.

I do have an e-mail address. Do you have one? Try creating yourself an e-mail

FIGURE 4-12 If Eukey has an e-mail address, do you think you can create one for yourself? If you do not know ask you teacher or your parents to help you.

What is the Web?

The **Web** is part of the Internet.

The is a collection of electronic documents

The Web has millions of Web pages.

Web pages have pictures.

Web pages have sounds.

Web pages have words.

FIGURE 4-13 This teacher takes her students into the lab to use the web.

What is the Web?

You can use the Web to get information.

You can get the news on the Web.

You can get the weather on the Web.

You can meet friends on the Web.

Many kids in Liberia love the Web

FIGURE 4-14 In this picture, the owner of tlcafricacom, the multipurpose website, Ciatta Victor helps a young lady navigates the Internet or the Net as it is called in Liberia.

Some Web pages change every day. Does your school have a Web pages?

FIGURE 4-15 Many schools in Liberia do not have a website. Can you answer the question Baby-E is asking your?

What is the Web?

You can work on the Web.

You can plan trips on the Web.

You can play games on the Web.

Moms and Dad can shop on the Web.

Students and teachers can work on the

Web

FIGURE 4-16 The City of Monrovia.

In the next few years, the Web is going to be a

big thing in Liberia with the help of the new Fiber

Optic Internet.

FIGURE 4-17 Symbol of shopping online in Liberia.

FIGURE 4-18 Students doing homework online in Liberia.

FIGURE 4-19 With the help of the Web, you may one day shop online in this supermarket.

How Do I Look at Web Pages?

To look at Web pages, you need to be online.

To look at Web pages, you need a **browser**.

A browser is a computer program.

There are many different types of browsers.

In Liberia, many people use **Internet Explorer** as their Web browser.

The Ministry of Education has a Web site and many Web pages.

FIGURE 4-20 A picture of Baby-E using her computer to go online. In this picture she is using Mozilla Firefox as her browser.

FIGURE 4-21 An illustration showing a computers online. Do you go online? Which Web browser do you use to go online.

What is a Home Page?

The **home page** is the first Web page you see when you start the browser.

The **home page** is also the first Web page you see when you visit a Web site.

The publisher of this book has a home page.

Does your school have a home page?

FIGURE 4-22 Students in computer lab.

FIGURE 4-23 The old Home Page of Clarke Publishing and Consulting Group, Inc .

What is a Home Page?

A **Web site** has Web pages that belong together.

Your school may have a Web site.

A store may have a Web site.

The government of Liberia has a Web site.

Companies in Liberia have their own Web site.

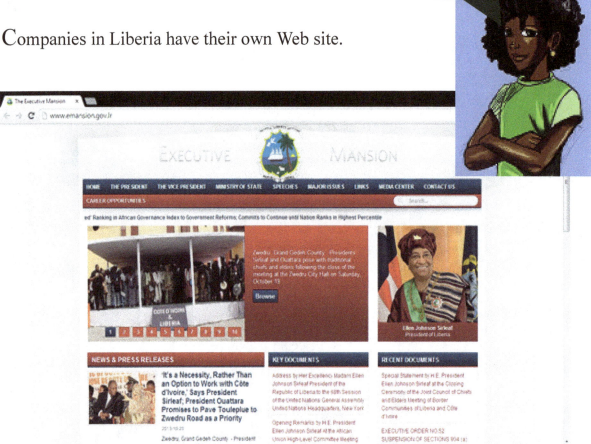

A Web site has Web pages

FIGURE 4-24 The website of the Government of Liberia, www.emansion.gov.lr has more than 50 web pages. Some websites can have hundreds of individual web pages.

What is a Web Address?

Each Web page has a Web address.

A Web address looks like this: **www.emmanuelclarke.com**

The computer uses the Web address to find the Web page on the Web.

To view the content of a Web site, you must know the Web address.

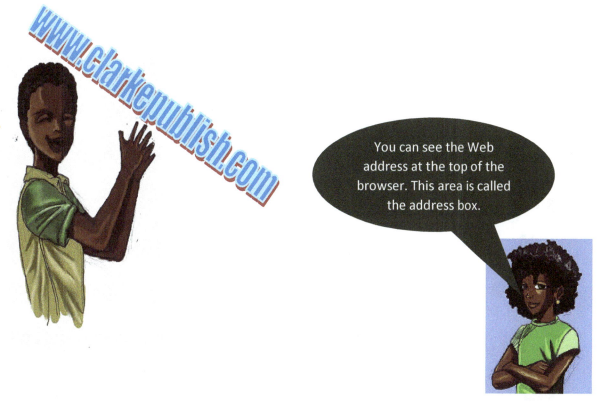

You can see the Web address at the top of the browser. This area is called the address box.

FIGURE 4-25 Every website has a unique Web Address. A Web Address is like a house address on a street. No two houses have the same number. This is the same thing with a Web Address, no two websites have the same address.

How to be Safe on the Internet?

The Internet can be fun for everyone.

Many good things are on the Internet.

Some bad things are on the Internet.

You have to follow rules to be safe.

Your teacher will help you learn these rules.

FIGURE 4-26 The Internet is a world different from ours. As a student, it is good to abide by Internet user rules to keep you safe. There are good and bad people on the Internet. Beware!

How to be Safe on the Internet?

Follow these rules when you use the Internet.

Your teacher is going to help you learn more rules about the Interne and the Web

Everyone must obey these rules in order to be safe while online.

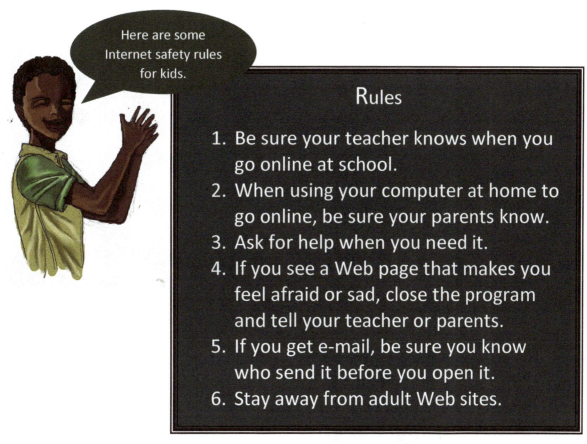

Here are some Internet safety rules for kids.

Rules

1. Be sure your teacher knows when you go online at school.
2. When using your computer at home to go online, be sure your parents know.
3. Ask for help when you need it.
4. If you see a Web page that makes you feel afraid or sad, close the program and tell your teacher or parents.
5. If you get e-mail, be sure you know who send it before you open it.
6. Stay away from adult Web sites.

FIGURE 4-27 The Internet is a wonderful world filled with billions of resources and information for everyone. As a student, it is good to abide by Internet user rules to keep you and the computer safe. Viruses are found on the Internet. A virus is a computer program that can cause damage to the computer. Bad people send virus infected e-mail to your e-mail box. Beware!

Looking at Web Pages

You have to go online to look at Web pages.

You use a browser to look at Web pages.

As stated earlier, there are different types of browsers.

FIGURE 4-28 These are some of the popular Web browsers people use to surf the Net.

Have you ever tried any of the Web browsers above? Go online and try each of them. You might just like one of them!

FIGURE 4-29 Luah's Favorite Web browser is Microsoft Internet Explorer. What is yours?

Looking at Web Pages

What You Will Do

You will start the browser to go online.

You will look at a home page.

You will click to see a new page.

What You Know How To Do

You know how to double-click.

You know how to scroll.

You know how to click.

You know how to close a program.

You know how to save a file.

Looking at Web Pages

GO **1.** Look at the screen.

Do you see the icons of the desktop?

2. Find the browser icon.

3. Double-click the browser icon. **STOP**

Find the browser icons on the desktop.

FIGURE 4-30 A Web browser is a user gateway to the World Wide Web. This desktop picture has several Web browsers icon. Can you identify them on this picture or on your own desktop?

Looking at Web Pages

To Look at a Web Page

GO **1.** Look at the screen.

Do you see the home page?

2. Look at the home page.

Do you see pictures of books?

Do you see words?

What other things do you see? **STOP**

You teacher will help you find other things on the home page.

Now remember, every Web site has a home page. 732-582-6651

FIGURE 4-31 This old picture of the home page of www.clarkepublish.com shows several books the company has in its catalog. What other things do you see on the home page?

Looking at Web Pages

You can click **links** on Web pages to go from one page to another page.

There are different types of links to Web pages.

Some links are words.

Some links are pictures.

FIGURE 4-32 This picture shows various types of websites connected together via chains. This is a typical example of how web pages are joined together by links or hyperlink.

Looking at Web Pages

GO **1.** Look at the pointer on the screen.

Does the pointer look like. 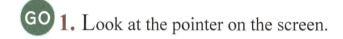 or

2. Move the pointer over the Web page.

3. Watch how it changes.

When your pointer looks like your pointer is on a link.

4. Click a link on the Web page.

Link

A new Web page is on the screen. **STOP**

On a Web page, anything can be a link.

FIGURE 4-33 Yes indeed anything can be a link on a web page, words, picture, etc.

Looking at Web Pages

To Go Back

GO **1.** Click

Back takes you back to the page you just saw.

The home page should be on your screen.

2. Click on a new link.

The Back button is on the top left row of the buttons. Can you find it?

3. Click **STOP**

FIGURE 4-34 The back and front arrows allow a user to easily navigate Web pages on the World Wide Web or Net.

Looking at Web Pages

Some Web pages are too big to fit in the browser's window.

To see the rest of the page, you need to scroll.

Do you remember how you did it in Chapter 3?

It is the same method you will use to view the Web page.

When you scroll, you see more of the Web page.

Can you try it now?

Drag the scroll bar down to scroll.

FIGURE 4-35 To see the entire page of a website that is too big, it is a good thing to scroll down the page.

Looking at Web Pages

GO **1.** Do you see the scroll bar on the side of the window?

2. Drag the scroll bar down.

Do you see more of the Web page?

It is easy to do with lots of practice! **STOP**

Did you do it?
Great job!

FIGURE 4-36 Depending on the size of the website you're viewing, always use your up or down scroll bar to navigate the page. This website www.clarkepublish.com has a lot of pages out of view on the computer. To view them, use your mouse or keyboard to move the page up or down just like Baby-E did.

Matching

Match the words to the pictures.

1. Internet

2. Web Page

3. e-mail address

www.clarkepublish.com

4. Web address

5. Back Button

info@clarkepublish.com

CHAPTER 5

The Keyboard

New Words

Backspace

Enter

home row keys

insertion point

keyboarding

Return

spacebar

symbol

type

Words You May Know

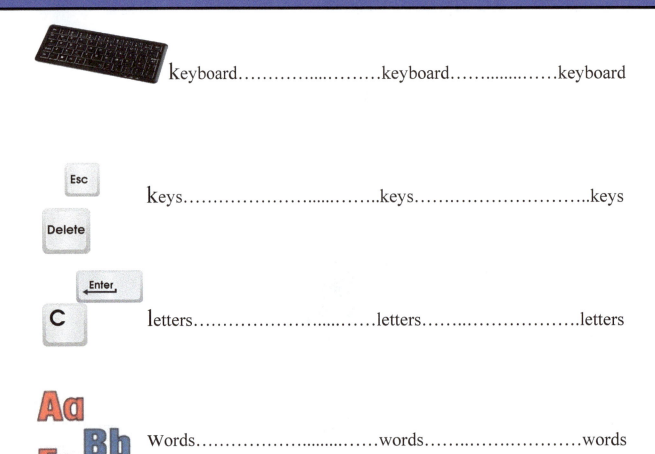

keyboard…………....………keyboard……........……keyboard

keys……………….....……..keys………………………….keys

letters……………….....……letters……..………………letters

Words……………….......……words……..………………words

Ask Clarke

Words You Will Learn

You will learn the right way to sit at a keyboard.

You will learn how to avoid health risk while using a computer.

You will learn the home row keys.

You will learn how to press keys.

FIGURE 5-1 Learning how to type on the computer keyboard is very important. It is a good thing to learn how to type on the keyboard.

What is a Keyboard?

A keyboard is part of a computer.

You use a keyboard to **type**.

A keyboard has letter keys.

A keyboard has number keys.

A keyboard has special keys.

"This keyboard has many pretty colored keys. Find the various keys of your choice." Savs Eukev

FIGURE 5-2 A keyboard enables a user to enter data an instructions into the computer. The computer keyboard comes in many different colors, sizes and shapes.

What is a Keyboard?

Some keys have numbers and **symbols.**

A symbol is a sign that has meaning.

Do you know what the $ symbol mean?

Some keys have words too.

Every kid in Liberia should learn to use the computer keyboard.

They also need to learn the various keys.

FIGURE 5-3 A keyboard is comprised of many different keys. Some keyboards have 123 key that contains various symbols and special characters.

What is a Keyboard?

When you press a letter key, the letter shows on the screen.

When you press a number key, the number shows on the screen.

When you press a key with a word **Enter**, the word does not show on the screen.

FIGURE 5-4 A computer keyboard allows a user to type letters and numbers. This 2nd Grader, Emmaree used her laptop to type letter to her father and mother and her favorite teacher at school. Can you use the keyboard to type a letter to your teacher or parents?

What is Keyboarding?

Keyboarding is using a keyboard to type letters.

Keyboarding is using a keyboard to type numbers.

Keyboarding is using a keyboard to type symbols.

To type, you press keys on the keyboard.

FIGURE 5-5 Keyboarding is the process of using the keyboard to type or enter letters and numbers into the computer. As a student, it is a good thing to learn how to use all of the keys on the keyboard.

Getting Ready to Keyboard

A computer has a keyboard.

You use the keyboard to types.

What You Will Do

You will learn how to sit at a computer keyboard.

You will explore the keyboard.

You will learn how to do many other things with the keyboard

FIGURE 5-6 A picture of a modern computer lab in the United States of America. While the computer lab in your school may not look like this one, with your current computer lab, you can type words using the keyboard or even a letter to your favorite teacher in your school. Can you name some of the things you can do with the keyboard?

Getting Ready to Keyboard

How you sit is called posture.

We sitting at the computer,

it is good to Sit up straight when

you use the keyboard.

FIGURE 5-7 A picture of Baby-E sitting at her computer doing her home work. Whenever you site at the computer, always make sure your lower back touches the back of the chair. by doing this, you will reduce back strains and muscle strains. If you sit the wrong way at your computer, you could damage your lower back nerves and this could cause you lower back and neck pains.

Posture is the first thing when it comes to using a computer.

Getting Ready to Keyboard

GO **1.** Be sure your hands are clean

whenever you use a computer keyboard.

FIGURE 5-8 Good posture makes all the difference. Practice it!

2. Sit straight or upright in your chair.

3. Look at the keyboard. What do you see?

Look at the picture above. Is the little girl sitting correctly? Whenever you sit at the keyboard to type, tap the keys gently. Ask your teacher to help you try this out. How did it go?

Getting Ready to Keyboard

The computer is on.

Look at the screen.

You are ready to use the keyboard.

To Explore the Keyboard

GO **1.** Look for the A key.

The Letters on a keyboard are not in ABC order.

2. Look for the B key.

FIGURE 5-9 Pictures of Computer keyboards with letter or alphabet keys being pressed. When you practice keyboarding, you could master typing on any computer keyboard.

Getting Ready to Keyboard

3. The spacebar is a long bar at the bottom of the keyboard.

FIGURE 5-10 Pictures of Computer keyboards with letter or alphabet keys being pressed. When you practice keyboarding, you will learn how to use many of the keys.

4. Find a key that has a word on it.

Getting Ready to Keyboard

The **home row keys** are the letter keys

 And the

The home row keys are where your fingers rest.

To Explore the Keyboard

GO 1. Look at the picture.

It shows you how to place your fingers.

One of the most important things in using a keyboard is knowing how to place your fingers on the keyboard.

Left   **Right**

FIGURE 5-11 Learning to type can sometimes be difficult, but if you as a student learns how to properly place your hands on the keyboard, try typing, it can be very easy. Just try as shown in this picture.

Getting Ready to Keyboard

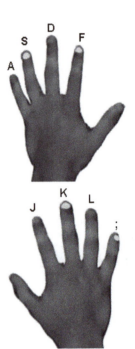

2. Place the tips of the fingers on your left hand on [A] [S] [D] and [F].

3. Place the tip of the fingers on your right hand on [J] [K] [L] and [;].

4. Place you thumbs on [⬜] STOP

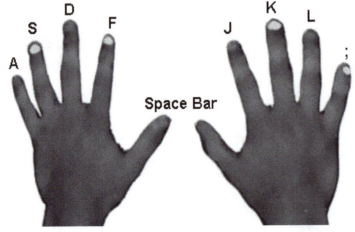

Space Bar

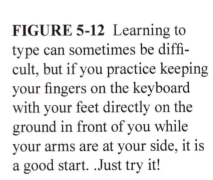

FIGURE 5-12 Learning to type can sometimes be difficult, but if you practice keeping your fingers on the keyboard with your feet directly on the ground in front of you while your arms are at your side, it is a good start. .Just try it!

Using the Keyboard

The blinking line on the screen is the insertion point.

The insertion point is where the letters you type show on the screen.

You Will Do

You will learn how to type letters.

You will learn how to make spaces.

You will learn how to make symbols too.

You will learn to do many things.

Using the Keyboard

To Type Letters

GO **1.** Place your fingers on the home row keys.

You have to keep both arms by your side.

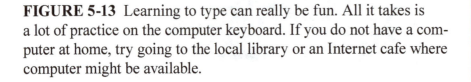

I hope you're ready to begin typing on the keyboard. Did you know typing is fun?

FIGURE 5-13 Learning to type can really be fun. All it takes is a lot of practice on the computer keyboard. If you do not have a computer at home, try going to the local library or an Internet cafe where computer might be available.

Using the Keyboard

First, you use the fingers on your left hand.

2. Press

The insertion point moved one space to the right.

3. Press

4. Press

5. Press

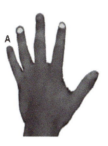

Insertion point

WOW! That was really cool. Let's try it again

FIGURE 5-14 The series of steps above are very simple. If you continue your practice by using the first eight keys on the keyboard, you will master using the other letters and other special keys on the keyboard.

Using the Keyboard

Now use the fingers on your right hand.

6. Press

7. Press

8. Press

9. Press

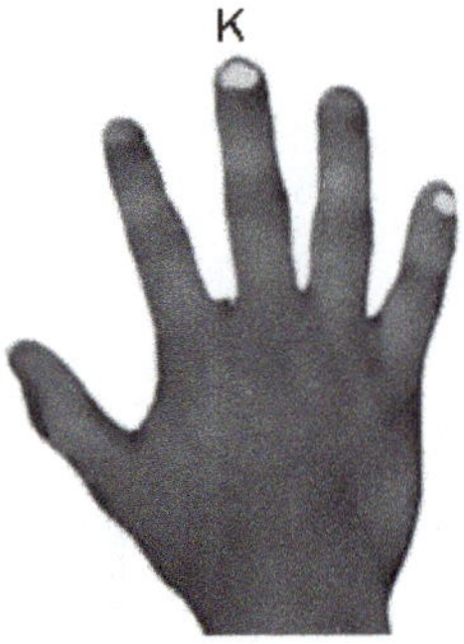

STOP

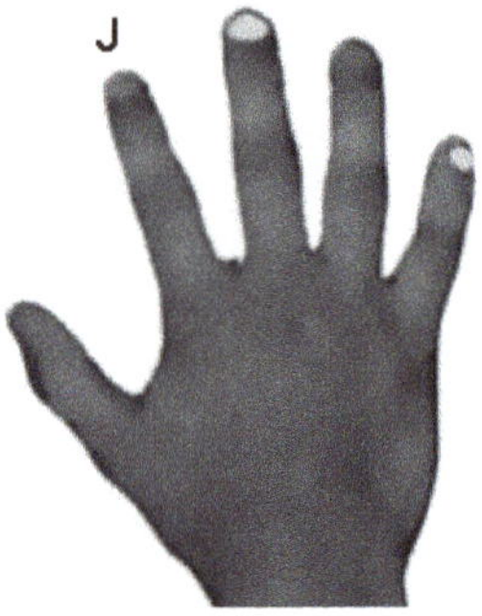

a s d f j k l ; |

Insertion point

Hey....You did it!

FIGURE 5-15 The series of steps above are very simple. Try doing it several times and you will see how easy it is to use the other keys.

Using the Keyboard

Look at the words on the page.

What do you see between the words?

You see spaces.

You press the **spacebar** to make a space.

To Use the Spacebar

 1. Place your fingers on the home row keys.

Use a thumb to press the spacebar. Did the insertion point move to the right? Good job my friend!

Using the Keyboard

2. Press ⬚A⬚ and then press

⬚⬚⬚⬚⬚⬚⬚⬚⬚⬚⬚ with your thumb.

The insertion point moved one space to the right.

3. Press ⬚S⬚ and then press ⬚⬚⬚⬚⬚⬚⬚⬚⬚⬚⬚

a s |

4. Press, ⬚D⬚ press ⬚⬚⬚⬚⬚⬚⬚⬚⬚⬚

5. press, ⬚F⬚ and then press ⬚⬚⬚⬚⬚⬚⬚⬚⬚

FIGURE 5-16 The series of steps above are very simple. The most simple is of them is the use of the spacebar which is done by the thumbs. Can you try using all ten fingers now? Good!

Using the Keyboard

Now use the fingers on your right hand.

6. Press, J and the press ▭

7. Press, K press ▭

8. press, L press ▭

and then press. ⦂ 🛑

Look at your screen? Does it look like mine? Yeah, you did it! Good Job!

FIGURE 5-17 The series of steps above are very simple. The difficult of all is the colon/semicolon key. But will little more practice, you can master it using your right pinky finer to reach that key.

Using the Keyboard

You can type the letter g.

The ⬚G⬚ key is in the middle row.

It is next to the ⬚F⬚ key.

When you press ⬚G⬚ you type the letter g.

To Type the Letter g

(GO) **1.** Place your finger on the home row keys

You use your left pointer finger to press the ⬚G⬚ key.

FIGURE 5-18 The letter 'G' is one of the easiest letters to type. Using your left pointer finger, you move it one stroke over to the right in order to reach the 'G' key.

Using the Keyboard

2. Lift your left pointer finger from

and press G

The letter g is on the screen.

3. Place your left pointer finger back on F

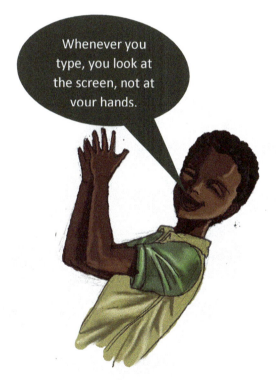

Whenever you type, you look at the screen, not at your hands.

FIGURE 5-19 The letter 'G' is one of the easiest letters to type. No matter if your write with your left or right hand, it is easy to reach the 'G' key on the keyboard.

4. Press and then press

You typed gg and then made a space.

5. Practice typing g and then a space. **STOP**

FIGURE 5-20 The letter 'G' is one of the easiest letters to type. The more you practice, the better you will get at using the letter 'G' and other letter/Alphabet keys.

Using the Keyboard

You can type the letter h.

The H key is in the middle row.

It is next to the J key.

When you press H you type the letter h.

To Type the Letter h

GO **1.** Place your fingers on the home row keys.

You use right pointer finger to press the H key.

FIGURE 5-21 The letter 'H' is the second easiest letters to type. Using your right pointer finger, you move it one stroke over to the left in order to reach the 'H' key.

Using the Keyboard

2. Lift your right pointer finger from J and press H

The letter 'h' is on the screen

3. Place your right pointer finger back on

Remember to always look at the screen, not your hands.

FIGURE 5-22 The letter 'H' is the second easiest letters to type. If you practice, you will get good at using the 'H' key along with other keys on the keyboard..

Using the Keyboard

4. Press H and the press

_____

You typed hh and then made a space.

Remember to press

_____ to make a space.

5. Practice typing **h** and then a space.

FIGURE 5-23 The letter 'H' is the second easiest letters to type. If you had followed the steps above, your screen should look like this. Does your screen look like this?

Using the Keyboard

For Liberian school kids, typing is fun.

Mastering typing takes a lot of practice.

What You Will Do

You will learn how to use the Enter

key or the Return key

You will learn to use the Backspace

key.

Starting to Type

The Enter key is a special key.

On some keyboards, it is called the Return key.

When you press the insertion point moves to the next line.

What You Will Do

GO **1.** Place your fingers on the home row keys.

2. Press **L** **A** **D**

3. Press **ENTER**

The insertion point

moved down to the next line.

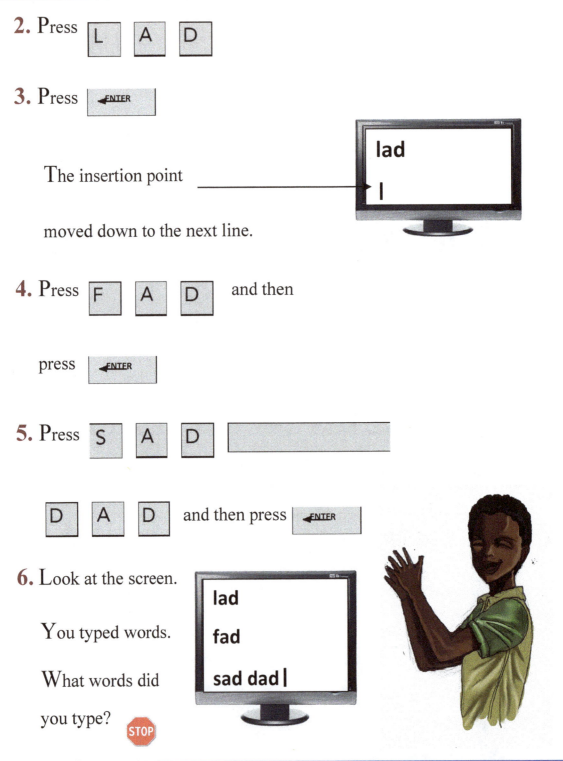

4. Press **F** **A** **D** and then

press **ENTER**

5. Press **S** **A** **D**

D **A** **D** and then press **ENTER**

6. Look at the screen.

You typed words.

What words did

you type? **STOP**

Starting to Type

The **Backspace** key is a special key.

You press the Backspace key to move back one space.

You press the Backspace key to erase one letter, number or symbol.

The Backspace key works like an eraser.

To Use the Backspace Key

GO **1.** Place your fingers on the home row keys.

2. Press A S K and press

C L A R K E

FIGURE 5-24 The Backspace button is the eraser for the computer. Whenever you're typing and make a mistake, all you have to do is put the blinking cursor in front of the letter or word and use the Backspace button on the keyboard to remove the mistake. Just try using it, and you will discover how useful it is.

Starting to Type

3. Press one time.

The last **e** is erased.

4. Press again.

The last **k** is erased.

5. Look at your screen.

Your screen has the seven words **ask Clar**.

You used to erase extra

letters you typed.

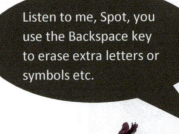

Listen to me, Spot, you use the Backspace key to erase extra letters or symbols etc.

FIGURE 5-25 The Backspace button is the eraser for the computer. It is a good idea to use it instead of the delete button. the Backspace button only erases one letter or character at a time.

Starting to Type

You can type more words.

To Type Words

GO **1.** Place your fingers on the home rows keys.

2. Types lad and then press

[   ]

3. Type fad sad dad.

Remember to press

[   ] to make the

space after each word.

FIGURE 5-26 Typing is very easy as long as you are comfortable with using the home row keys, "A S D F, and J K L ;". The Spacebar helps to separate typed words.

Starting to Type

4. Press 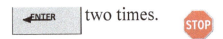 two times.

5. Type have a nice day and then press

ENTER two times. STOP

Great! You just typed yourself words. Keep practicing to type.

Matching

Match the words to the pictures.

1.

2.

3.

4.

INDEX

PHOTO CREDITS

A SPECIAL THANK YOU!

Dear Student:

It was a great pleasure serving you. We look forward to meeting you in the not so far future. Please do not forget to access course and other educational materials from our website at: www. clarkepublish.com. Once there, you should click the "Support" link. On the Support page, kindly navigate to "Growing Up With Technology" link. There are lots to interact with on our site.

While this might be it for now, we hope to meet you again when you begin your Junior and Senior high journey. For us at Clarke Publishing and Consulting Group, Inc. we want to be a part of your academic success. This is why we'll be with you every step of the way until you can make it through high school and into university or college.

Thank you for choosing us as your technology learning partner.

The Clarke Team